# Nanu the Pol

By Genie Lai

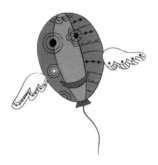

Nanu the Polar Bear Moves / by Genie Lai
Illustrated by Genie Lai
Advisor by Associate professor Chia-Hua Chu
English Translation by Mei-Hsien Wang
Copyright © 2011 by Genie Lai. All rights reserved.

Nanu the Polar Bear lives on the beautiful and milky white sea ice of the Arctic Ocean where snowflakes keep swirling in the freezing cold winter.

When snowflakes stop drifting, Nanu, who has slept throughout the whole winter, wakes up in spring.

It is a time for him to have fun in skiing.

Nanu hunting his favorite Ringed Seals.

However, it is unusually hot this year and days grow longer. Nanu can't help but licking a melting popsicle.

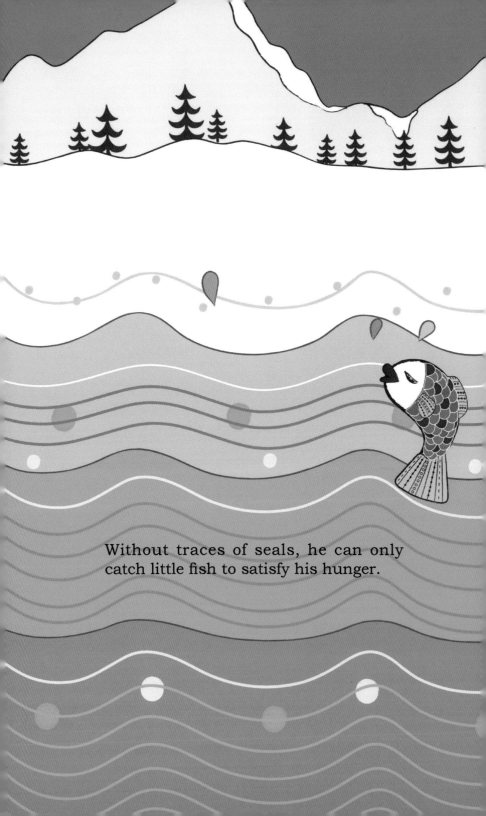

Without traces of seals, he can only catch little fish to satisfy his hunger.

The heat of the warmer weather melts
the igloo he lives in. He can't believe
what he sees and is terrified.

Nanu finds that the magic balloon his mother left isn't being swept away, so he grabs it right away.

With his beautiful milky white home fading away, Nanu rides on his magic balloon. He decides to fly all over and to explore the world, at the same time, to look for a new place to live. He wants to make new friends.

Bears of the World

"We are *TUAN-TUAN and *YUAN-YUAN the Giant Panda. We have a cozy new house in Taipei Zoo. We can eat bamboos and snacks as much as we want. Though everyone likes us, we still miss friends back in our hometown—mountains in Sichuan. Our home gets taken over by development, pushing us into smaller and less livable area. We can't easily find a perfect bamboo forest to live."

*TUAN YUAN is a Chinese term for gathering together

Giant Panda's Home

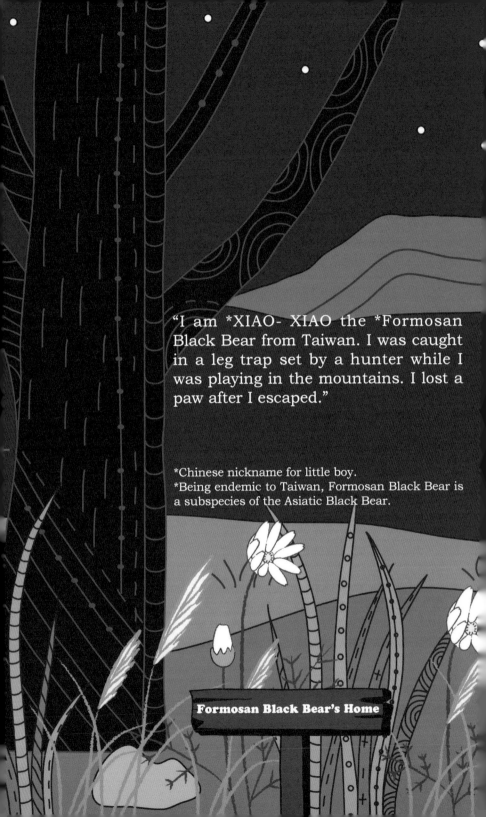

"I am *XIAO- XIAO the *Formosan Black Bear from Taiwan. I was caught in a leg trap set by a hunter while I was playing in the mountains. I lost a paw after I escaped."

*Chinese nickname for little boy.
*Being endemic to Taiwan, Formosan Black Bear is a subspecies of the Asiatic Black Bear.

**Formosan Black Bear's Home**

"I am *XIONG MEI the Sun Bear. I live in the tropical rainforest which is the most important place for lowering the temperature of the earth. Keeping cutting trees from the rainforest, people make a big trouble for Earth—global warming."

*Chinese nickname for younger sister.

**Sun Bear's Home**

"I am Kenny the American Black Bear. It's getting warmer and warmer while the sweet ripe wild berries are getting less and less. My stomach always rumbles because I am hungry all the time. Now I have to climb higher and walk farther in the mountains to look for food, satisfying my hunger."

American Black Bear's Home

"I'm Leo the Brown Bear. It is supposed to be cool in October but it is still hot now. I don't know why. I feel sleepy and keep yawning all the time, but I can't fall asleep.

**Brown Bear's Home**

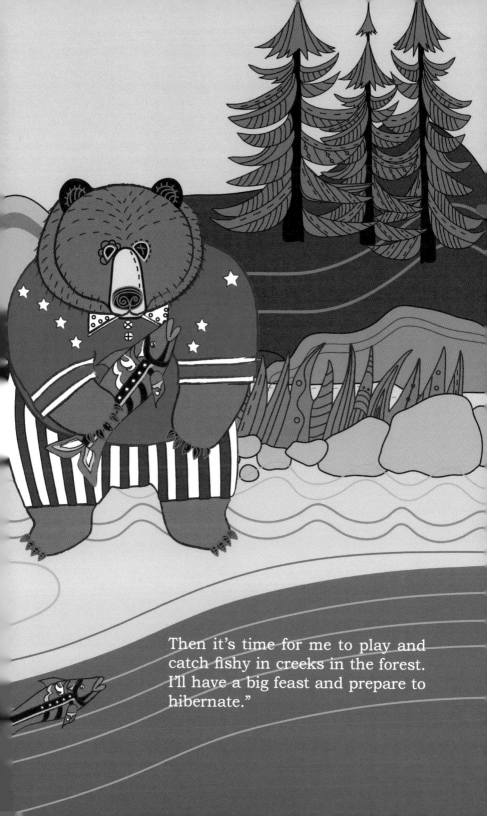

Then it's time for me to play and catch fishy in creeks in the forest. I'll have a big feast and prepare to hibernate."

"I am *XIAO TIE the Spectacled Bear. People are cutting down trees from the forest I live in. I have to move to the Andean Forests which is high in the mountains and is covered with cloud and fog all year. People are rarely seen here. I only come out for food until the night falls, the whole forest dozing off."

*Chinese nickname for strong boy.

Spectacled Bear's Home

"I am *BUPU the Sloth Bear. I learn dancing in the circus. I dance crazily on the stage and laughter from the audience fill the room. After the performances end, I look afar into the forest in silence. I think I hear my mom sighing softly."

*Chinese nickname.

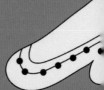

So Nanu the Polar Bear keeps
moving on, wandering off.

Printed in Great Britain
by Amazon